HYMNS OF THE FAITHFUL SERIES

# PENTECOST
# TRINITY

LEADERS GUIDE

WRITTEN BY

Richard Resch

CPH
Concordia Publishing House

# Contents

HYMN 1
Beautiful Savior                                        *Page 4*

HYMN 2
Praise God, from Whom All Blessings Flow    *Page 7*

HYMN 3
Praise to the Lord, the Almighty                  *Page 8*

HYMN 4
Holy Spirit, Ever Dwelling                          *Page 10*

HYMN 5
Baptized into Your Name Most Holy            *Page 11*

HYMN 6
Holy God, We Praise Your Name                 *Page 13*

---

Series editor: Thomas J. Doyle

This publication is available in braille and in large print for the visually impaired. Write to the Library for the Blind, 1333 S. Kirkwood Rd., St. Louis, MO 63122-7295; or call 1-800-433-3954.

All Scripture quotations are from the HOLY BIBLE, NEW INTERNATIONAL VERSION®. NIV®. Copyright © 1973, 1978, 1984 by International Bible Society. Used by permission of Zondervan Publishing House. All rights reserved.

Copyright © 1999 Concordia Publishing House
3558 S. Jefferson Avenue, St. Louis, MO 63118-3968
Manufactured in the United States of America

1  2  3  4  5  6  7  8  9  10     08  07  06  05  04  03  02  01  00  99

# Introduction

The Hymns of the Faithful Bible study series provides participants the opportunity to study in-depth favorite hymns and Christian songs. This CD pack contains two of a series of six studies.

The leaders guide includes background information concerning the text and tune for some of Christendom's most beloved hymns. Each session in the leaders guide includes the following sections:

- **Textual Source(s)**–provides the scriptural sources the author used in writing the hymn.
- **The Hymn's Text**–provides information concerning the author of the hymn and the context in which the hymn was written.
- **The Hymn's Tune**–provides information concerning the tune associated with the hymn, including who wrote the tune and alternate uses of the tune.
- **Tradition about the Hymn**–describes the way in which the hymn has been used by the church.
- **The Confession of Faith Sung in This Hymn**–describes the theological truth(s) that the hymn confesses.

The study sheets are designed for use in a class or small-group setting, but may also be used by individuals for their personal devotions. Every session has a separate study sheet. Each of the reproducible study sheets includes activities and questions to guide the participant into an understanding of the basic theological truths confessed in the hymn and to assist the participant in applying these truths to life. Each study sheet includes the following sections:

- **Focus**–introduces the participant to the concepts that will be explored during the session.
- **Inform**–provides questions to guide the participant into a deeper understanding of the scriptural truths confessed in the words of the hymn. This section may be supplemented by the leader with information found in the leaders guide.
- **Connect**–provides activities and questions to help the participant apply the truth found in the words of the hymn to life.
- **Vision**–suggests activities for further devotional use of the hymn during the week to come.

In addition to the leaders guide and the study sheets, an audio CD includes a musical, sing-along version of the hymn. Use the audio CD to accompany your class or small group in singing the hymn at the beginning of each session. You may also want to play the hymn as participants arrive and/or depart from class.

May God bless the study of His Word proclaimed in the words of some of the church's favorite hymns.

# Session 1

# Beautiful Savior

*Textual Sources:*
*Isaiah 4:2–6; Psalm 48:2*

## The Hymn's Text

This text first appeared in a manuscript from Münster, Germany, in 1662 and was first printed in the Roman Catholic *Munsterisch Gesangbuch* in 1677.

## Translation

The anonymous translation that begins "Fairest Lord Jesus" is used in most hymnals, other than Lutheran hymnals. In those hymnals, the hymn appears as follows:

*Fairest Lord Jesus, Ruler of all nature,*
*O Thou of God and man the Son,*
*Thee will I cherish, Thee will I honor,*
*Thou, my soul's glory, joy, and crown.*

*Fair are the meadows, Fairer still the woodlands,*
*Robed in the blooming garb of spring;*
*Jesus is fairer, Jesus is purer,*
*Who makes the woeful heart to sing.*

*Fair is the sunshine, Fairer still the moonlight,*
*And all the twinkling, starry host;*
*Jesus shines brighter, Jesus shines purer*
*Than all the angels heaven can boast.*

A Lutheran pastor by the name of Joseph A. Seiss translated the familiar "Beautiful Savior." It was first published in the *Sunday School Book for the Use of Evangelical Lutheran Congregations* (Philadelphia, 1873). This translation is found in all present-day American Lutheran hymnals.

## The Hymn's Tune

There are two tunes and three tune names associated with "Beautiful Savior." The three names are SCHÖNSTER HERR JESU, CRUSADER'S HYMN, and

ST. ELIZABETH. The tune names seem to be interchangeable with the two tunes. Most Americans are unfamiliar with the original tune, which is still known and loved today in Germany.

The tune familiar to most American Lutherans is from the Glaz district of Silesia. The noted poet and scholar Heinrich Hoffmann von Fallersleben wrote a folk melody as he heard it sung by haymakers in 1839. He then published the tune in a collection of sacred and secular folksongs from Silesia, *Schlesische Volkslieder,* in 1842. The famous American "Beautiful Savior" tune first appears in print in this collection. Some believe that the folksong of the haymakers has as its roots a set of variations by Wolfgang Amadeus Mozart (K. 24).

## Tradition about the Hymn

"Beautiful Savior" is not included in the hymnals of all major denominations. Many who do include it use the alternate text: "Fairest Lord Jesus." In fact, it is not easy to find commentaries on this hymn in the highly respected sources of hymnody because it is not considered a major hymn by many denominations. "Beautiful Savior" clearly does not have the same revered status in other denominations as it does for Lutherans.

The St. Olaf Choir has made "Beautiful Savior" famous throughout the world. For many decades the choir has sung "Beautiful Savior," as arranged by F. Melius Christiansen, at the end of their concert-tour programs. It therefore has become the signature piece of this world-renowned choir and appears regularly at the end of their broadcasts, tapes, and CDs.

## The Confession of Faith Sung in This Hymn

"Beautiful Savior" is the voice of the faithful confessing with awe and reverence some of the characteristics of their beautiful Savior. He created them and saved them; He is the light of their soul, their joy, their crown. He is God; He is man; He is Lord of the nations. He is brighter and purer than the stars and the angels. He makes their sorrowing spirits sing. In faith, Christians also sing their response to His saving love: love Him, serve Him, and give Him glory, honor, praise, and adoration now and forevermore.

Hymnal commentaries frequently refer to this hymn as a distinctively Lutheran hymn. While it is a beautiful text and tune combination (with either tune), it is not a distinctively Lutheran confession.

Hymn singing is an integral part of the church's preaching and teaching (Colossians 3:16; Ephesians 5:19–20). Therefore, a high standard is required for this activity. For hymn singing is not just a pleasurable part of the Christian's life together with other saints (although it is definitely that), but it is a significant form of proclamation of the Gospel of Jesus Christ that shapes belief from cradle to grave. Singing will therefore always point to the saving work of Jesus Christ. Singing confesses to God what He has first done for us, what He is now doing, and what He promises to do for us into eternity. The faithful sing frequently about such doctrines: the forgiveness of sins, Baptism, the Lord's Supper, and the theology of the cross.

## Session 2

# Praise God, from Whom All Blessings Flow

*Textual Sources: Psalm 146; 147; 148; 149; and 150*

## The Hymn's Text

The doxological words "Praise God, from whom all blessings flow" begin the concluding stanza of Thomas Ken's morning hymn "Awake, My Soul, and with the Sun" and his evening hymn "All Praise to Thee, My God, This Night." As Ken prepared *A Manual of Prayers for Use of the Scholars of Winchester College* in 1674, he suggested the use of three hymns for "morning," "evening," and "midnight." He later wrote such hymns and published them in 1692. His morning and evening hymns are now in widespread use in English hymnals. However, the last stanza, "Praise God, from Whom All Blessings Flow," has been separated from the original text and lives on in great popularity throughout the world.

The text is a doxological stanza that praises the Father, Son, and Holy Spirit. It has the nickname "The Long-Meter Doxology," which simply means there are four lines of eight syllables each.

## The Hymn's Tune

The tune name, OLD HUNDREDTH, was composed by Louis Bourgeois and was first included in the *Trente quatre pseaumes de David* (Genevan psalter) in 1551 as the musical setting for Psalm 134. In the 1561 edition it was wed to William Kethe's version of Psalm 100. Hence, the title, OLD HUNDREDTH.

This text is also sung to the familiar tunes MORNING HYMN and TALLIS' CANON.

## Tradition about the Hymn

"Praise God, from Whom All Blessings Flow" is one of the few hymns that pastors dare to ask people to sing from memory in virtually any setting. It may be the most known and memorized hymn in all of Christendom. People commonly break into four-part harmony when singing this beloved hymn.

## The Confession of Faith Sung in This Hymn

In this text all creation in heaven and on earth praise and adore God—Father, Son, and Holy Spirit. As singers confess, they acknowledge the source of all blessings: the Triune God—Father, Son, and Holy Spirit. It is a highly condensed version of the outburst of praise that occurs at the end of the Book of Psalms.

# Praise to the Lord, the Almighty

*Textual Sources:*
*1 Chronicles 16:23–36; Ezra 3:11; Nehemiah 9:6;*
*Psalm 91:4; 103:1–11; 150; and Isaiah 40:21*

## The Hymn's Text

"Praise to the Lord, the Almighty" was written by Joachim Neander and was published in Bremen in 1679. Neander is sometimes called the "Paul Gerhardt of the Calvinists." Neander's original text is a five-stanza version. A four-stanza version is common in most English hymnals.

## The Translation

The famous Catherine Winkworth (1829–78) translated this hymn. It was published first in her *Chorale Book for England* in 1863. Although not a Lutheran, Catherine Winkworth dearly loved the Lutheran chorales and spent much of her life translating these German hymns (chorales) into English.

## The Hymn's Tune

The tune name is called LOBE DEN HERREN. Neander adapted a tune he found in the *Erneuerten Gesangbuch* (Stralsund, 1665). His original version was quite different from what we now know. The present form is first found in Winkworth's *Chorale Book for England*. J.S. Bach used this hymn tune in his Cantatas 57 and 137 and in the well-known Schübler Chorale no. 6, "Kommst du nun, Jesu."

## Tradition about the Hymn

This is clearly one of the best-loved hymns in all of Christendom. It gloriously weds text and tune into a hymn that is easy to learn and memorable. The text is general enough that it can serve at anniversaries, services of thanksgiving, and almost any Sunday morning. It has even been sung at funerals.

## The Confession of Faith Sung in This Hymn

"Praise to the Lord, the Almighty" is an expanded version of "Praise God, from Whom All Blessings Flow." Here the faithful sing specifically of God's many gracious gifts. It seems as if all of creation is caught up in this song. The loud "amen" does not wait for the end but is included within the body of the hymn.

If this hymn has a weakness, it is that it does not speak clearly about God's work for us in Christ Jesus—namely, His sacrificial death on the cross through which we receive the forgiveness of sins and eternal life. The strongest hymns typically go beyond the First Article of the Apostles' Creed and focus on the Second Article—God's atoning work on our behalf through the person and work of Jesus Christ.

## Session 4

# Holy Spirit, Ever Dwelling

*Textual Source: 1 Corinthians 2:9–16*

### The Hymn's Text

This two-stanza Pentecost text written by Timothy Rees, Bishop of Llandaff, first appeared in a four-stanza form in his *Merfield Mission Hymn Book* (London, 1922). In 1946 it was published by Rees in a three-stanza, greatly altered form in *Sermons and Hymns*. The two-stanza form (stanzas 2 and 3 of the original) first appeared in the *Church Hymnary*, third edition (London, 1973). This is the form most familiar to American Episcopalians and Lutherans in their hymnals.

### The Hymn's Tune

The tune is called IN BABILONE. It is first found in a 1710 collection of old and new Dutch peasant songs and country-dances. Many of these were published again and arranged in 1912 by the distinguished Dutch pianist and composer Julius Rötgen. Ralph Vaughan Williams, who served as music editor of the 1906 *English Hymnal*, saw this tune and included it with the text "See the Conqueror Mount in Triumph." However, the tune is now connected frequently with the text "Holy Spirit, Ever Dwelling."

### The Hymn's Tradition

This hymn continues to gain popularity in all denominations for use on Pentecost Sunday.

### The Confession of Faith Sung in This Hymn

Martin Luther wrote, "We must not doubt that the Holy Spirit dwells in us. We must be sure and acknowledge that we are a 'temple of the Holy Spirit' (1 Corinthians 6:19). For if someone experiences love toward the Word, and if he enjoys hearing, speaking, thinking and writing about Christ, he should know that this is not a work of human will or reason but a gift of the Holy Spirit" (from Lectures on Galatians, 1535).

This text is extremely comforting since it clearly states the work of the Holy Spirit in the life of the individual and the life of Christ's church. It provides a strong confession of the faith. The church sings here what Scripture teaches regarding the third person of the Trinity.

## Session 5

# Baptized into Your Name Most Holy

*Textual Sources: Matthew 28:19–20; Galatians 3:26–29*

### The Hymn's Text

This text is written by Johann Jakob Rambach (1693–1735, a University of Halle professor of theology). Rambach wrote more than 180 hymns. "Baptized into Your Name Most Holy" is one of eight included in *Erbaulisches Handbuchlein für Kinder* (Giessen, 1734). It originally had seven stanzas.

### The Translation

Catherine Winkworth translated six of the seven stanzas and included them in her *Chorale Book for England*. Some hymnals include all six stanzas, while others include only four stanzas.

### The Hymn's Tune

The tune name is O DASS ICH TAUSEND ZUNGEN HÄTTE. Obviously, the tune name does not come from this Baptism text, but rather from the familiar hymn "Oh, that I Had a Thousand Voices." The melody was written by Kornelius Heinrich Dretzel, and it first appeared in *Des evangelischen Zions musicalische Harmonie* (Nuremberg, 1731). Dretzel became the organist of the Nuremberg *Frauenkirche* at the young age of 14. He was organist at several famous German cathedrals throughout his life. His 1731 chorale collection was the most complete collection published up to that time.

### Tradition about the Hymn

This glorious hymn is usually sung before, during, or after the baptismal order by the faithful gathered to witness this most significant event.

### The Confession of Faith Sung in This Hymn

Martin Luther wrote,

> *Since Baptism is a divine act in which God Himself participates and since it is attended by the three exalted persons of the Godhead, it must be prized*

*and honored. One must agree that Baptism was not invented by any mor-*
*tal but was instituted by God. It is not plain water but has God's Word*
*in it and with it; and this transforms such water into a soul bath and into*
*a bath of rejuvenation. (from Sermons on the Gospel of St. John,*
*1537–40)*

This entire hymn is spoken in the first person singular. Yet it is not an individual's subjective statement of what is happening here, but rather what all of the faithful can objectively stand and confess together regarding the sacrament of Holy Baptism. In this hymn we confess the scriptural teachings about Holy Baptism—its significance, its power, its blessings. The hymn can be sung any day of a person's life as a remembrance of her or his Baptism.

# Holy God, We Praise Your Name

*Textual Sources: Psalm 30:1–4; 105:1–4; 111:2–9;*
*Isaiah 6:2–3; Luke 2:13–14; and Revelation 7:9–12*

## The Hymn's Text

This text is a German versification, *"Grosser Gott, wir loben dich,"* of the Latin *Te Deum laudamus.* It appeared first in the *Katholisches Gesangbuch* published in Vienna in 1744. The author is not known, but the hymn has enjoyed immense popularity and is included in virtually all the major Christian hymnals in the United States.

## The Hymn's Translation

The translation is by Clarence Augustus Walworth (1820–1900) and was first included in the *Catholic Psalmist* (Dublin, 1858).

## The Hymn's Tune

The tune is also anonymous. It has the tune name GROSSER GOTT (also TE DEUM).

## Tradition about the Hymn

The Te Deum (We praise You, God!), in one form or another, has been used and present at all the major events of the church for approximately the last 1,500 years.

"Holy God, We Praise Your Name" is a well-loved hymn in Roman Catholic churches. It was played as the late President John F. Kennedy's casket was carried out of St. Matthew's Cathedral in Washington, D.C., on November 25, 1963. It was also sung by a large crowd at Yankee Stadium in New York City following the historic celebration of the Mass by Pope Paul VI on October 4, 1965.

Because this hymnic setting of the Te Deum is easier to learn and sing than the prose setting accompanied by Anglican chant, it is often used as a way to introduce the Te Deum to a congregation. The Te Deum is the canticle appointed for the Office of Matins, and this form could be used there.

## The Confession of Faith Sung in This Hymn

The Te Deum is a creed of the church. Martin Luther considered the Te Deum second only to the Apostles', Nicene, and Athanasian Creeds as

---

a confession of the Christian faith. It confesses all the most important doctrines of the Christian Church in a concise way.